Tufu Yama:
Tufu to the Rescue

TUFU YAMA

VEGETARIAN EXOTIC MEALS FOR HEALTH

Tufu Yama: Tufu to the Rescue.
Copyright © 2021 by Carlos Nobles.

All rights reserved. No part of this book may be reproduced in any form or by any electronic or mechanical means, including information storage and retrieval systems, without permission in writing from the publisher and author, except by reviewers, who may quote brief passages in a review.

This publication contains the opinions and ideas of its author. It is intended to provide helpful and informative material on the subjects addressed in the publication. The authors and publisher specifically disclaim all responsibility for any liability, loss, or risk, personal or otherwise, which is incurred as a consequence, directly or indirectly, of the use and application of any of the contents of this book.

Certain stock imagery © Shutterstock.com.

ISBN: 978-1-63950-111-3   [Paperback Edition]
       978-1-63950-112-0   [eBook Edition]

Printed and bound in The United States of America.

Gateway Towards Success

1309 Coffeen Avenue
STE 1200, Sheridan,
Wyoming, 82801 USA
+13179780258
www.writersapex.com

TUFU YAMA

TUFU TO THE RESCUE

Carlos Nobles

TUFU YAMA

VEGETARIAN FOOD AND JUICE

STRENGTHENING FOOD FOR YOUR HEALTH,

MIND, AND BODY

Table of Contents

Introduction 9

Squash Fu 19
Soy Burger Fu Mushroom 21
Mango Fu 23
Pumpkin Chocker /Soy 25
Okra Fu 27
Soy Fu 29
Bean Fu 31
Cushah Sauce 33
Carlos's Curry Rice 35
Rice & Peas / Carrots 37
Veggie Enchiladas 39
Peach, Yams and Bananas 41
Veggie Spaghetti With Soy Protein 43
Veggie Pizza 45
Veggie Harvest 47

LIVITY TO

Haile Selassie

* **

SPECIAL THANKS TO

My instructor, Ras Zet, and The Sami' Family

* **

DISCLAIMER

The information contained in this book is expressed as the author's opinion based on extensive research he has conducted. However, this information is not intended to be used as a medical diagnosis or prescription for any physical or mental ailments. Anyone seeking medical advice should personally meet with a qualified health practitioner.

INTRODUCTION

I'm coming to you live and direct from the kitchen of Tufu Yama. I want to talk to you about nature's food. Getting in touch with your body through the earth, spices that cleanse your mind and soul. But first, I want to give thanks to Jah, The Creator and the people of the West Indies for inspiring me to learn these wonderful techniques of their wonderful way of cooking.

I first found out about this food when I was in Prairie View A&M University. And there were the people of the island. But it was not until I came back to San Antonio when I met people from Trinidad and I really learned how to cook the food and became more familiar with the custom of cooking the food. At first when I tasted the food, I thought it was very different so I took it slow at first then I tried several other dishes. I used a lot of avocado and wheat bread, soy margarine and those things at that aspect which are very much healthy and inspiring to everyone. So, as I went on trying different dishes, I got so interested in learning how to prepare my own meals at home. So I could have food for myself and my family. I went on and learned more about it, and finally got on to cooking. It didn't come overnight and you couldn't learn it just by someone telling you.

If you don't have direct recipes or hands on experience then it would be very hard to obtain by just someone telling you how to do it. So I got the hands on experience and I learned how to cook it. And the food came out somewhat okay I thought but you have to cook it a while and learn how to sauté' the vegetables neatly stewing them through and through stirring occasionally, making sure there's a nice sauce level. And then after a while you will get the concept down pat. And then you move on to being official, and your meals taste exactly the same way as the champion bubbler. That's when I began creating my own dishes and letting people try them and they liked my food and they wanted to have more of my food. These recipes will help people to prepare my food at their own home. We want to reach the public and people who never had the chance to visit the islands or ever be acquainted with people from the islands that can cook this certain way. This is my work, it's something I love to do ... cook. It's one of my favorite things to do besides music. When I cook I find it very relaxing and these meals they aren't rush -rush meals.

However, they can be prepared in a short amount of time. Make sure everything is correct and taste your meal as you go and you will find out that taking it easy makes the food come out a lot better. I've taught people how to cook like this also and they've gone on to become very good cooks. I like their dishes also. They've even created their own dishes. And I like that. Makes me feel good knowing that I showed someone and they went on to be inspired like I did to create their own dishes and become more health-conscious. The food will make you more prosperous and if you have lack of energy it will certainly build that for you as well. You will be strong and will be able to have a good day full of activity. So I advise everyone if you're overweight; if you're slim; if you're healthy; if you're strong, weak, old or young, I advise everyone to take timeout some time and try out some of these dishes. This food can make you look good, feel good, and give you better concentration 'cause you feel wholesome. That's why I like to use fresh vegetables when preparing my food.

Whole vegetables contain all the natural juices that it has reaped from the earth which will make you feel wholesome and strong. When you find out more about these recipes and you might want to take it upon yourself to invest in things of consciousness such as the music, it carries a message. I like the music, The Island music, Reggae music, African music and Caribbean music. It sort of goes together with this West Indian food. You can relax, think better and be in touch with nature. Sometimes you just want to use

fresh vegetables to create the dish. Once you become accustomed to doing this, often you will find that it's not complicated, it's not expensive, and it's guaranteed to make you feel a lot better. You can do almost anything if you eat right. You always have to think of your body first by filling it with good essentials, vitamins, herbs and spices. Herbs are very important with these dishes. A person can take these recipes and really spice it up by using more spices if they like. It will enhance the flavor. There's a sauce out there called "cuchilu." It's a mild sauce made with mango peels and hot sauce. You can get it at the International Food Market. It's made in the Caribbean and in the West Indies. This sauce goes very well with this food. If you can't find it, you're okay with just these simple recipes.

If you're eating right, you're feeling right. If you want a meal cooked, you'll soon be able to come to my restaurant. Always try to eat right every day from morning to night whether it's fruit, veggie snacks, fresh juices like coconut juice or orange juice. All these things are very good for your body. In my recipes, I use soybean products which are very good for your body also. Remember you can't drink enough juices like orange juice …or any other juice that's 100%. This is jungle food. Jungle foods are bananas, oranges, grapefruits, plums and apples. We want to stay on this type of diet. Why? Anytime you want to be prosperous in your life whether on your job, with your family, or wanting to make sure you're eating right, these are the meals you need to eat. So, hook up a little something from this book. You might want to make a veggie harvest or maybe a veggie pizza. Any of these will make you feel just fine. You won't find this everywhere, but once you try these foods, they will heal your body.

So, at this kitchen, the Tufu Yama Kitchen, we are always in the pots. If we're making curry rice or if we're making peaches, yams or bananas, we're always in the pots. We try to keep a nice variety of something on hand. Just in case we want to try something different the next day like veggie enchiladas; we just use soy protein, onions, tomatoes, tortillas, black olives, tomato sauce, lemon and pepper seasoning, curry seasoning and camino. So this is an excellent way to a healthy and prosperous life. We serve this with rice & peas and carrots. Try to use coconut milk with a lot of these dishes. When we blend these together, (we carefully measure to make sure you get the right flavor) use soy margarine, basil, thyme and garlic seasoning. If you want more of a certain seasoning, it's okay. I just advise you to taste it as you go. Anytime you feel like you want to cook up something, or you just want to make something simple, try some of these recipes. Their very easy to prepare. And like I say, these dishes are fun. Cooking is fun. It's not anything that's so hard to do. If you feel like cooking is slavery, it's really not. Cooking is an experiment and also you will be rewarded with something you created yourself and you get a chance to get other people's opinion. A lot of times, you might not know clearly how to make certain things so you might need to follow some recipes until you

can completely understand how this food is cooked. And more and more, we see West Indies food appearing, arising and satisfying more and more Americans everyday. From grapefruit to veggie burgers, all these things are included in our natural foods.

Today people want to eat right, they want to eat healthy. They also want the food to taste good. The food is excellent but you have to get accustomed to it first like I did about 15 years ago because I wasn't raised in the islands (I was born in America.). When I traveled and became interested in how they ate to make them feel so strong, and be so healthy, I acquired it. I tasted it and it was different. I wasn't use to it, so I took it slow. I couldn't finish the first dish I had because it was so new to me. But I felt so clean when I ate the food. All food is clean, don't get me wrong. It's just that it has a natural connection with nature because you're using perishable vegetables and seasonings galore which are fresh from the earth. And from the majoram to lemon pepper even curry, you got all these seasonings, that you can learn how to put together. You collect seasonings and you learn what seasonings would go good with certain meals.

Not all seasonings go with any meal. But when you are cooking peas, and rice curry is an excellent seasoning for rice. Chili powder is an excellent seasoning for peas and beans. So you want to be familiar with what seasoning goes with what food. It's not hard. Once you start with these simple recipes then you're on your way to identifying just what seasonings go with what vegetables. Once you acquire that taste, and understand that it is possible to create and serve delicious meals quite often, it's so much fun and healthier for you. I'll advise anyone who wants to be health-conscious, come together with friends. Learn and understand the simple methods of having very good essential meals that will create an atmosphere for yourself and your friends and family. A unity amongst everyone in the community. Cook a dish for someone or try it yourself. Try never to walk alone with nature. In Tufu Yama's Kitchen, we always try to create a different dish. We always try to stick to the basics about twice a week. We always seem to have room to create more dishes because there's so many types of vegetables and seasonings that it broadens the vocabulary and the mind to herbs you've never even heard of unless you've gone to the herb section of the store. You'd have to go to a health food store because some stores aren't fully prepared in that area. They may have a few but you find more in health food stores. You eat right, you live right. And we always try to focus on being helpful to everyone to make sure everyone is feeling good.

If you see someone and they aren't feeling good, you can learn how to prepare these dishes well, or maybe take then a dish. Let then try it. I guarantee you it will bring a smile. This food not only feeds you but it heals you. Herbs are tomatoes, onions, carrots. I can go on naming vegetables that prevent illnesses. They will heal and they will cut down the doctor bill. So you might want to keep in mind of how many ways that these dishes help to enhance your life with the lifestyle that you live. When I cook and eat the food, it makes me want to play music and dance. It makes me strong. It's vegetarian food which is vital and is well appreciated in the Rasta community as well as by vegetarians all over the world. We want to introduce this food and make sure you understand it. Expose yourself to the food and stay experienced with the food. From Tufu Yama's exquisite vegetarian kitchen and health-conscious awareness, we want to brighten the hearts and minds of everyone. This is ngozi mangozi. Thank you for supporting us!

SET UP TO MOST DISHES IN FIVE EASY STEPS

STEP 1: Add Garlic

STEP 2: Add Onions

STEP 3: Chop Celery

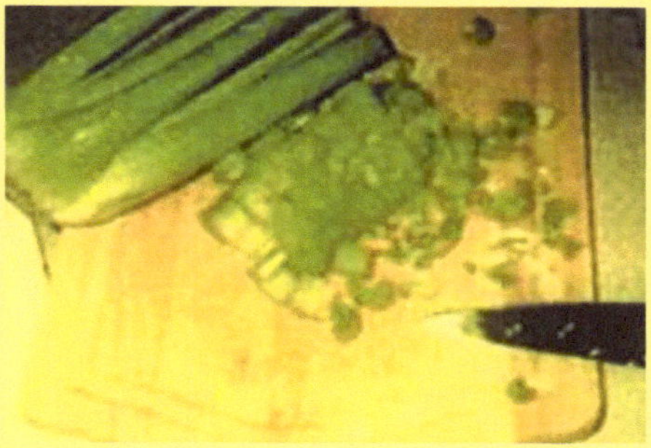

STEP 4: Add Celery

STEP 5: Add Tomatoes

SQUASH FU

1	Palm garlic	3	Yellow Squash
3	onions	4 tsp	Curry powder
4	tomatoes	2 tsp	Cumin
¾	stalk celery	1 tsp	Cayenne
¼	bunch green onions	1 stick	margarine
4 Tbsp.	Canola oil	1 tsp	Thyme
3 ½	Tbsp. Black pepper	2 tsp	Oregano
3	Zucchini Squash	4 Tbsp.	Canola oil

In large pot heat medium temperature. Add oil, peel garlic, let brown, peel onions; slice thin. Slice celery in thin slices add. Bruse green onions slice thin add, take Zucchini squash slice thin add, yellow squash slice thin add, slice tomatoes add + margarine let simmer 5 min add all seasonings cook 20 min. add ½ cup water stir simmer 10 mins.

SOY BURGER FU MUSHROOM

½ lb.	Soy Burger or two patties	2 ½ tlbsp.	Curry Powder
¼ lb.	Mushroom	3 tlbsp.	Garlic + herb
3	Onions	1	Avocado
3	tomatoes	1	Plaintane
1	palm Garlic	2 tlbsp.	Oregano
3 tlbsp.	Canola oil	2 tlbsp.	Cumin
1 stick	butter or margarine	4 tsp	Olive oil
½ stalk	celery		

Heat dry pan till hot add oil let heat then peel garlic add, slice onion thin add, slices celery in thin slices add, slice mushroom add. Let simmer 15 min. Tell sauté then add seasonings stir add tomato sauce. Then soy Burger let cook 10 min. Peel + slice plantain in thin slices, in small skillet heat add olive oil, brown on both sides. Let drain on paper towel. Serve Fu over Rice plantain on top slice avocado.

MANGO FU

3	mangos	1 tsp	Cayenne pepper
3	Onions	3 tlbsp.	Cumin
4	tomatoes	1 stick	margarine
¾	stalk celery	1 tsp	Thyme
¼ bunch	green onions	4 tlbs.	Canola oil
4 tlbsp.	Black pepper	3	Yellow squash
3	Zucchini squash		
3 tblsp.	Cilantro		

In large pot heat med temperature. Add oil, peel garlic add let brown, peel onions; slice then. Slice celery in thin slices. Add bruise green onions slice thin add, take Zucchini squash slice then add, yellow squash slice thin add, slice tomatoes, add peeled mangos and carve meat off the seed and margarine, let simmer 5 minutes add all seasonings. Cook 20 min. Add ½ cup water. Stir and let simmer 10 minutes.

PUMPKIN CHOCKER /SOY

2 lb.	Pumpkin or whole Pumpkin squash	1	palm garlic
1 ½	stick soy margarine	3	tomatoes
2 tblsp.	Vegetable oil	3	onions
2 tblsp.	Basil	½	cup of water
2 tblsp.	Cumin	2 tbsp.	Black pepper
2 tsp	Soy sauce		
2 tlbsp.	Lemon herb		
1 tsp	Curry		

In large pot add oil, add peeled garlic, brown on both sides. Add peeled and sliced onions. Add sliced tomatoes and let simmer for 5 min. Add margarine, Slice seedless pumpkin and add all seasonings while stirring in pot. Add water and simmer for 20 mins.

OKRA FU

1 lb.	Okra	2 tlbsp.	Basil
3	onions	2 cans	tomato sauce
4	tomatoes	1 stick	Butter
1 palm	garlic	1 tlbsp.	Cumin
½	celery stock	2 tlbsp.	Lemon + herb
1 bush	green onions		
4 tblsp.	Canola		
2 tblsp.	Curry		

Preheat pot med. Temp. peel and add garlic. Brown and add thin-sliced onions. Add sliced celery stock and let cook for 5 mins. Slice + dice tomatoes, add sliced green onions, add ¼ inch sliced okra. Stir in butter and all seasonings. Simmer for 20 min.

SOY FU

2 lbs.	Tofu		3 Tbsp.	Curry
2 tsp	Cumin		1 palm	Garlic
3	Onions		2 tlbsp.	Marjoram
4	Tomatoes		2 tsp	Chili Powder
½	Stalk Celery		2 tlbsp.	Lemon + Herbs
1 bunch	Green Onions		1 can	Tomato Sauce
4 tlbsp.	Vegetable oil		1 tsp	Red Pepper
2 Soy	Burger Patties		2 tlbsp.	Garlic Powder

In large pot add oil heat medium temperature. Add peeled garlic and thin sliced onions. Add sliced celery. Mash and slice the bunch of green onions. Let simmer 10 minutes. Slice tomatoes and soy patties and stir in all seasonings in with it. Add ½ cup of water and let simmer for 20 minutes.

BEAN FU

¼ lb.	Pinto beans	2 tblsp.	Marjoram
¼ lb.	Red beans	2 tblsp.	Lemon + herb
¼ lb.	Black bean	2 tblsp.	Sweet basil
¼ lb.	Black eyed peas	3 tblsp.	Chili powder
¼ lb.	Carrots	2 stick	soy margarine
2 soy	burgers	1 tsp	Canola oil
1 can	coconut milk		

In large pot add beans + peas. Fill with water and soak for 30 mins.

Empty and refill pot and bring to a boil and add coconut milk. After another 30 mins, add sliced carrots and continue cooking for another 30 minutes. Add 2 sticks of soy margarine and 2 soy burgers and boil for another 25 min. Add all seasonings and stir in well until beans, peas and carrots are soft. Enjoy this over rice with wheat bread.

CUSHAH SAUCE

2 large	Cushah
1 can	Coconut Milk
3 tblsp.	Allspice
1 cup	Honey
4 Tbsp.	Ginger
4 tblsp.	Herb + Spice

Take the two large cushahs and cut into it and take the insides out. Slice into chunks and put in large pot with coconut milk and the water 2 inch above level. Boil for 45 min. then add ingredients. Wait 5 minutes and stir in honey then cool and serve.

CARLOS'S CURRY RICE

2 cups	Rice
3 tblsp.	Curry Powder
1 ½ tsp	Honey
1 Stick	Butter
1 ½ tsp	Ginger
1 can	Coconut Milk

In medium-size pot, add the cup of coconut milk and add water to bring level to 2 inch over rice then boil for 15 minutes. Stir curry in and add ginger, honey and butter. Simmer on low temperature for 5 minutes or until soft then serve.

RICE & PEAS / CARROTS

2 cups	Rice
2 cups	soft or fresh Peas
½ stick	Soy Margarine
1 tsp.	Garlic Seasoning
3	Carrots
2 tsp	Basil
1 tsp	Thyme

In large pan, add carrots and water to put at 2 inch above carrots and boil for 15 minutes. Add rice and water to make 2 inch above rice. Let boil for 15 minutes. They add peas, seasonings and butter. Cook 10 minutes and serve.

VEGGIE ENCHILADAS

1 lb.	Protein	1 tsp	Lemon & Pepper
1	Onions		Any Fitting Seasoning
1	Tomato		
1 Package	Tortillas		
1 tsp	Cumin		
1 cup	Black Olives		
2 can	Tomato Sauce		

In large pan, place protein and sliced onions to pot along with sliced tomato sauce. Add seasoning and cook 15 minutes. Stir then Simmer 5 minutes. Heat tortillas in 1 by 1 in pan with light oil then roll one large spoon ½ protein ingredients after all or half is prepared. Set large cook sheet. Place and heat.

PEACH, YAMS AND BANANAS

1 can	Peach
1 can	Yam
1 ½	Bananas
2 Tbsp	Honey
2 tlsp.	Cinnamon
½ stick	Butter
1 tsp	All Spices

In large pot, add peaches and yams and simmer for 10 minutes. Add sliced bananas and butter, then add seasonings and honey and serve.

VEGGIE SPAGHETTI WITH SOY PROTEIN

2 lb.	Long Pasta
1 lb.	Protein
1	Onion
2 can	Tomato Sauce
2 tbsp.	Curry Seasoning
2 Tbsp	Oregano
1 tsp.	Basil
2 tblsp.	Lemon & Pepper

In large pot fill ¾ full of water and add pasta. Boil until soft, slice and dice onions. Take protein soy mix with seasonings and onions and form into balls. Brown and add to pasta. Warm tomato sauce and serve over protein and pasta.

VEGGIE PIZZA

12 inch	Pizza Dough	2 cans	Tomato Paste
1	Onion	3 cups	Shredded Cheese
2	Tomato		
1 ½	Tbsp Curry		
Lemon & Pepper			
½ cup	Stalk Celery		
2 Tbsp	Garlic Powder		
1 cup	Black Olive Slices		

Place 12 inch pizza dough on cookie sheet spread tomato paste on dough. Then shake shredded cheese evenly over paste, slice onions and spread over cheese. Slice celery in thin slices and spread over ingredients. Sprinkle olive slices over ingredients. Slice tomato in circle and lay in around formation.

VEGGIE HARVEST

2	Yellow Squash
1	Eggplant
2	Onion
3	Tomatoes
½ bunch	Celery
1	Bell Pepper
3 Tbsp	Canola oil
½ Stick	Butter

In large skillet, preheat at medium temperature. Add oil, slice squash, egg plant, onion, bell pepper, celery. Add to skillet and stir while cooking. Add butter and simmer 5 minutes. Serve over rice or on toast.

Stay fit, get fit
Food is the stepping stone
To life each and every day
Health is the key to happiness
Which everyone should have
At some point in life to achieve
Things and have things
Fu means "Forward Universal"
Soybean is the plant of the future
which many great things are formed
Peace and Blessings